Easter How to Draw

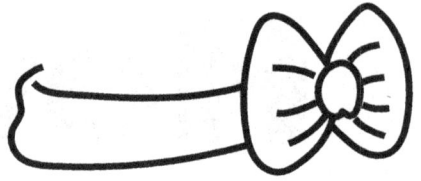

Try it yourself!

Try it yourself!

Try it yourself!

Try it yourself!

Try it yourself!

Try it yourself!

Try it yourself!

Try it yourself!

Try it yourself!

Try it yourself!

Try it yourself!

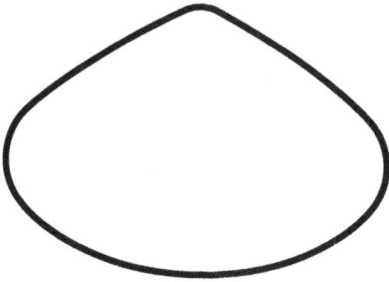

Try it yourself!

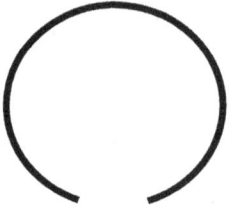

Try it yourself!

Try it yourself!

Try it yourself!

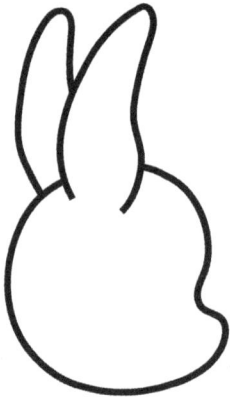

Try it yourself!

Try it yourself!

Try it yourself!

Try it yourself!

Try it yourself!

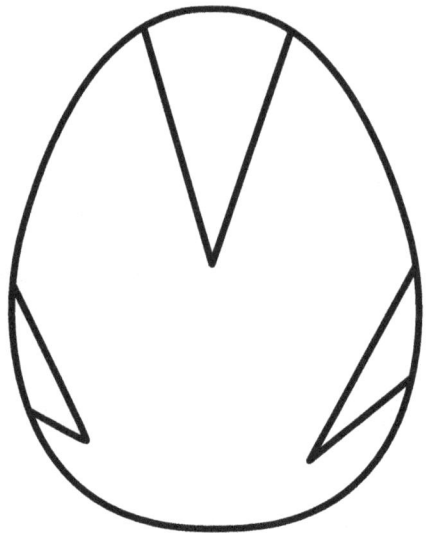

Try it yourself!

Try it yourself!

Try it yourself!

Try it yourself!

Try it yourself!

Try it yourself!

Try it yourself!

Try it yourself!

Try it yourself!

Try it yourself!

Try it yourself!

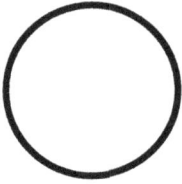

Try it yourself!

Try it yourself!

Try it yourself!

Try it yourself!

Try it yourself!

Try it yourself!

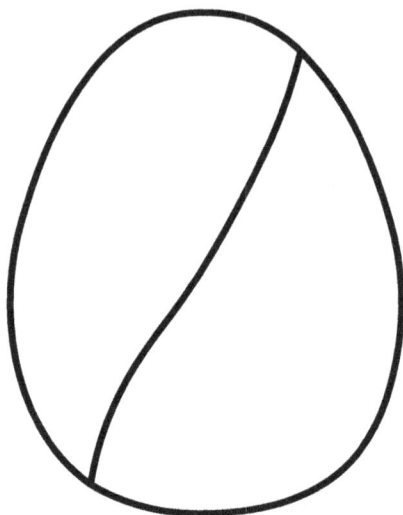

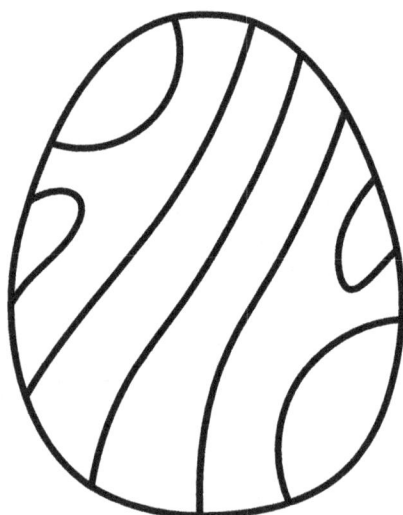

Try it yourself!

Try it yourself!

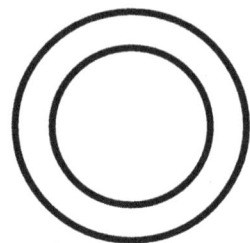

Try it yourself!

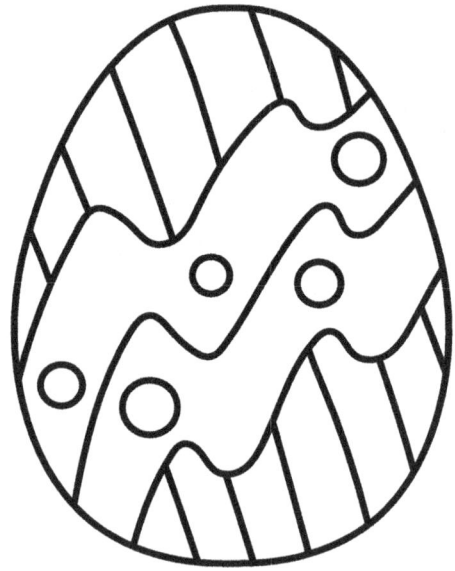

Try it yourself!

Try it yourself!

Try it yourself!

Try it yourself!

Try it yourself!

Try it yourself!

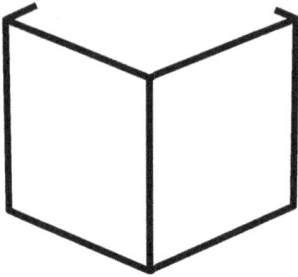

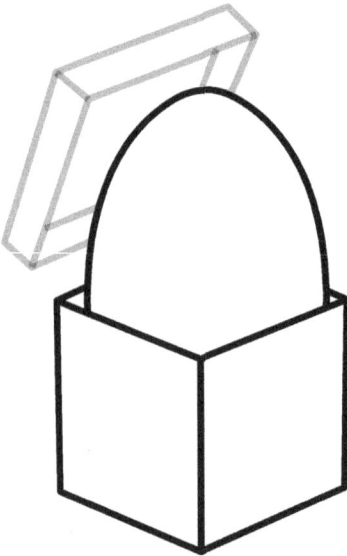

Try it yourself!

Try it yourself!

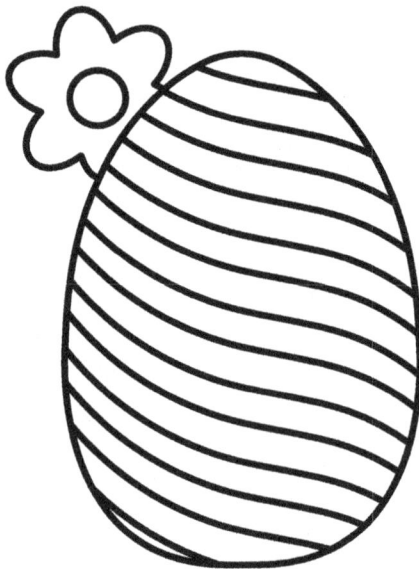

Try it yourself!

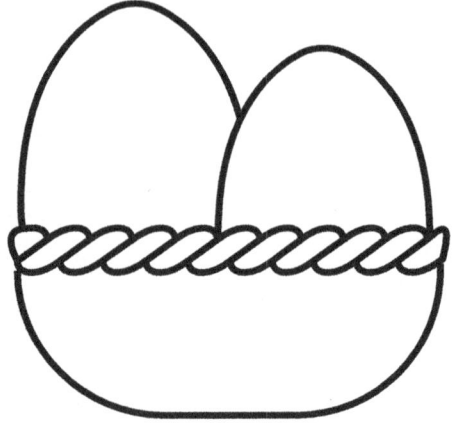

Try it yourself!

Try it yourself!

Try it yourself!

Try it yourself!

Try it yourself!

Try it yourself!

Try it yourself!

Try it yourself!

Try it yourself!

Made in the USA
Las Vegas, NV
29 January 2025